River Revery

Also by Penn Kemp

POETRY
P.S. (with Sharon Thesen, forthcoming), Fox Haunts, Local Heroes, Barbaric Cultural Practice, From Dream Sequins, Pinceladas (with Gloria Mulcahy), Re: Animating Animus, Poemas Escolhidos de Penn Kemp/Selected Poems, C'Loud, Sarasvati Scapes, Gathering Voices (with Gloria Mulcahy), Suite Ancient Egypt, Vocal Braidings (with Patricia Keeney), Incrementally, Throo, Eidolons, Some Talk Magic, Travelling Light, Animus, Binding Twine, Toad Tales, Changing Place, Clearing, Tranceform, Bearing Down

DRAMA
The Triumph of Teresa Harris, The Dream Life of Teresa Harris, What the Ear Hears Last, Angel Makers, The Epic of Toad and Heron

PROSE
What Springs to Mind, Four Women, The Universe is One Poem

Edited by Penn Kemp
Women & Multimedia, Performing Women, Jack Layton: Art in Action, Poem for Peace in Many Voices, Vol. 1 & 2, CVii: Spiritual Poetry in Canada, Twelfth Key, IS 14

River Revery

Penn Kemp

INSOMNIAC PRESS

Library and Archives Canada Cataloguing in Publication

Title: River revery / Penn Kemp.
Names: Kemp, Penn, 1944- author.
Description: Poems.
Identifiers: Canadiana (print) 20190190949 | Canadiana (ebook)
20190190973 | ISBN 9781554832385
(softcover) | ISBN 9781554832422 (PDF)
Classification: LCC PS8571.E4485 R58 2019 | DDC C811/.54—
dc23

The publisher gratefully acknowledges the support of the Canada
Council for the Arts and the Ontario Arts Council.

Printed and bound in Canada

Insomniac Press
520 Princess Avenue, London, Ontario, Canada, N6B 2B8
www.insomniacpress.com

THE CANADA COUNCIL | LE CONSEIL DES ARTS
FOR THE ARTS | DU CANADA
SINCE 1957 | DEPUIS 1957

ONTARIO ARTS COUNCIL
CONSEIL DES ARTS DE L'ONTARIO

For Ula & Kai and their generations

We begin in dream and then we move, down the stream....

Contents

Foreword

Poetry is a conversation with the consecration of self. It is the layman's law of the mind, a form of divinity open to all races and all peoples. This harvest of humanity is truly ancient and sometimes only lingers on in names, because they are the last to go behind the closing veil of history.

To the Western world, the word *Thames* is a mystery that even a sage cannot solve. In the past, places like the routes of rivers were known to everybody. And language always held a clue, especially in oral culture. The River Thames of London, England leads us back to Sanskrit (as Penn Kemp writes). It leads me back to a childhood trauma when I dropped my doll into its muddy waters, lost forever with my bitter tears. To Penn Kemp and the people of Southern Ontario, it reminds them of their heritage in 'stealing' a name for their beautiful home.

Poetry also refreshes the dream. So sit by the trees of your Carolinian forest, and make a wish. I will join you in this. Wishes lead to hope. Hope leads to action. So let's hope that the waters of *River Revery* can feed the forests of blue ash, *Fraxinus quadrangulata*, whose blue dye was once used in the popcorn wedding baskets for the First Nations of Canada. Let us all wish and hope together that we can protect this environment for Ula and Kai. Amen.

Diana B. Beresford-Kroeger is a medical biochemist, botanist, and the author of *To Speak for the Trees* and *The Global Forest*.

Tracking Souwesto Seasons

Given climate change catastrophe, how can a book of poems ever help? I've dedicated *River Revery* to my grandchildren, in the hope that they and their generation maintain love of our dear Earth, recognizing the need to find and enact solutions to imminent upheaval.

The river Thames winds through the city of London, Ontario, forking into two streams; thus, it was named Askunessippi, "the antlered river," by the original Algonquin inhabitants. For local Indigenous communities, it is Deshkan Ziibiing or "Antler River." French explorers called the river "la tranche," the ditch. Its current name derives from its colonial progenitor, a river goddess called *Tamesis,* the Celtic word for "dark flow." The name is a palimpsest: in calling the river a familiar, comforting name from the Old Country, English settlers colonized the forbidding new territory. The name reflects life as a pale imitation of 'home,' rather than embracing the vibrancy of this river as it is. The Thames waters my gardens, real and imaginary, "with real toads in them."

My own contribution is personal, from a garden's perspective. I'm interested in exploring the natural world as it impinges on urban realities. These poems illustrate the challenge of living in a setting which can overwhelm nature with mechanical stimuli. Outside my window, jackhammers awaken the day, digging up a city road to reveal an underground stream. Medway Creek, at the end of my street, flows into the Thames, which swallows it whole and continues through the city and on, to debouche into Lake St. Clair, Lake Erie, and the Atlantic Ocean.

Politicians have long turned their backs on the Thames, to our loss and the river's detriment. But London is coming to appreciate the river and its influence in practical terms, in new and exciting projects. The poems in *River Revery* reflect the changes in this river, how industry and agriculture have sullied it, and how it is being cleaned up. As a poet deeply involved with this particular place and cultural community, my ongoing concerns are best expressed in Ecopoetics, with its emphasis on ecology. Poetry is my defense against intrusive forces when political exigencies collide with the natural environment that so desperately needs protecting. A distillation of such experience, I hope, will lead to active solutions. Contemplation is not enough, nor is poetry. But it is a start, an *influence* (from Latin: a flowing that affects human destiny). Such inspiration is one source for right action.

Water is a metaphor for change through its many states from liquid to steam, mist to ice, all streaming. Rivers are often used to represent boundaries; to "cross the river" is to undergo a transformation. As the Greek philosopher Heraclitus remarked, "You cannot step into the same river twice, for fresh waters are ever flowing in upon you." Now comes the confluence of many streams of thought.

In her enchanting novel, *Once Upon a River*, Diane Setterfield writes: "And now, dear reader, the story is over. It is time for you to cross the bridge once more and return to the world you came from. This river, which is and is not the Thames, must continue flowing without you. You have haunted here long enough, and besides, surely you have rivers of your own to attend to?"

We do. And so our story begins, with London, Ontario's Thames, Deshkan Ziibiing, Askunessippi, "the antlered river."

To respect the longstanding relationships of the three local First Nations groups of this land and place in Southwestern Ontario, we would like to acknowledge the history of their traditional territory. The Attawandaron (Neutral) peoples once settled this region alongside the Anishnaabe, the Haudenosaunee, and the Leni-Lunaape peoples. This land was their traditional beaver hunting grounds. My home in London Ontario is on this territory, which also covers lands connected to the London Township Treaty and Sombra Treaty (1796) and the Dish with One Spoon Wampum. I live in the house I grew up in, on land I revere for its long history, and am grateful to be a guest here.

Penn Kemp
August 4, 2019

River Revery

Water abounds here, with this river

five times normal width for winter,
flooding roads and parks. The swell
carries whole trees along stampeding

currents. Yellow willows drop fifty-year
-old boughs in high winds. Standing
waves cover our usual walking path.

Climate change is certainly upon us,
from eleven below to eleven above in
hours, sinking back below freezing.

Green begins to bury the remnants
of flood, the wall of last fall's leaves
packed level against the link fence.

Weird how all reverts, reverberates in
spring clarity as old detritus is dredged.

My rant runs along the river in
long twilight along the shore, a
migratory route for warblers
alighting in cottonwood, a trill

unknown we cannot now locate
since sound is not where sight is
and the willows are leafing out.

Leaving out the paw-tracked mud,
the grocery cart obliterated by winter
storm back to origin, a mess of
twisted rust like an old fishing weir.

The current courses by standing waves,
standing in momentary eddies against
momentum.

True Cost: Walmart versus Woodland

This prose poem was written as a rant to be read at rallies and published in print and in audio.

Smart!Centres (Walmart) applies
for London zoning bylaw changes

so they can establish a Complex at
the corner of Meadowlily Road South

and Commissioners East right next
to Meadowlily Woods' last stand,

that *Environmentally Sensitive Area*
close to the Thames. Deep pockets

vie against deep wood. Development
vs. organic diversity. Tarmac vs. trillium.

What do you love? The choice is yours,
in season— Nature's long cycle or fake

hype selling discounted bargains months
before due date. Veracity vs. voracity.

The tag I gleefully paid can't account
for inevitable recompense in lost resource.

And the consequence? Invasive species
multiply in a virus of corporation logos

that we collect and prize in vain, while
native plants die out. Not a good deal.

What we don't know, we can't care for.
Meadowlily Woods' worth is now in flux.

How do you evaluate a loss of habitat
tamped down by asphalt, crushed by

power complexes where brand names
replace the reality of life that feeds us?

Smart!en up, Walmart. Opposing this
 development, I should not shop there

but low prices are a necessity for many.
How to work out such a conundrum?

What do we pay for the irreplaceable
place if it's lost? Memories all too soon

are boxed in by big stores selling greed.
Nostalgia like guilt is a sop to be sold.

"What's a Meadowlily?" kids will ask,
reading a street name, its reality lost.

What do we tell them when simulacra
of names replace the fullness of life?

How better appreciate the natural world—
changing, wild, free and our only home?

Ask what lasts. Glacial meltwater carved
a spillway through the Ingersoll moraine,

flood plain to terraced loam to upland clay,
Carolinian and northern Great Lake forest.

Over ten thousand years, so many species
found their place, settled, and now co-exist.

Native phlox and poppies from an old farm.
Willows sun-sparkle green on warbler song.

Beech on the hill slope shelter spring beauty.
Hemlocks mingle over fern in lacy ravines.

A boy wades into the river, fixing his lure to
wait, just as still as nearby great blue heron.

What cost beauty? What value do we place
on trail walks through harmonious complexity?

Property may appreciate in real estate value,
but we appreciate nature in real value.

In woods, you can breathe deeply and be
inspired. Here we know we belong, participating

in the co-creative process of simply living,
sensing continuous wholeness. Drawing

on the energy of nature, we emerge renewed
in a relationship of respect, understanding

what a wood is worth. Stand your ground!

Cautionary Tales

A flood plain should remain
untouched but foolish/ greedy
developers insist your basement
won't flood, won't flood, won't—
until water fills all holes full.

Ice floes we'd ride
down the mad March
current, slipping between
the elements, where
slush meets candled ice
meets freezing water.

Soakers galore but no
falling in. We drip home.

Cracks in Everything

All for Art

The photographer takes me down to the river,
my favourite spot. I dress up, thinking to just
stand by the bank and recite a poem while he

shoots. But no, he wants me by the water so
we scramble down the steep bank, brushing
back willow branches. He holds them back,

grinning: "I won't let them snap till you're
past." "Do you happen to have sisters?" I
ask, recognizing the temptation he resists.

The scene at water's edge is idyllic, replete
with Asian fisherman on the opposite bank,
an ancient sycamore bone white in the marsh,

raccoon tracks in the clay mud. Above us,
cottonwood shimmers, alive with twittering
pine warblers on the move north. Canada
geese follow a flight path the river clears.

For such an immersive experience, standing
on the edge won't do. I offer to wade in,
rolling up my pants like Huckleberry Finn,
giving my all for Art as
always. Early May

but the water's not freezing. Book in hand,
I read poem upon poem while the cameraman
creates a kaleidoscopic swirl of imagery from
sky reflected rippling in water, soft new green.

Happy to be a kid with the boys again, I
scuttle back up the bank, accepting a kind
hand. Back on the path, I point out birds
but neglect to notice the pit that last week's
flood dug out of the trail. Once again, I am
levelled with the elements, sprawled against
the earth, facing stone silence after the crash.

A fall so fast but slow the rise, humbly slow.
The stumble home in shock, strained restraint.

My bad knee scraped, the other ankle turned
unseemly. Now I watch their lovely video,
foot iced and bound, swollen and pounding.

When the photographer calls, I relay my state
of sprain. "Ah," he says. "Since you were in-
jured in the service of the River Project, you
can call your fall Performance Art." Well.

It's been done before, you know, labelling
The Fall. So we are escorted out of Eden.

So we transmute blessing into *blesser*, to
wound. When we have gone beyond our
bounds, we are bound to be bound but not
gagged. What limit will lift over the edge

from tension to attention? Attention to where
the videopoem starts with a poem's first line—
"I will bring you to the brink..."

Our Heads in Old Sand

The scene confirms our
worst fears—that things
are not what they seem.

A lurid summer postcard
allures tourists to false security
where nothing is safe.

Sinkholes drop us down
over our heads into
undertows of memory.

We are lifted high, flailing
astonished into the past, caught
by divers, diverse diviners.

Frantic, we fall through
streams of light, swirling blind,
gasping, riding the wave back

to when weekend fathers taught
us how to swim by plunging us
off the raft and mothers watched

benignly from the beach in those
far-off days when the river was
fit to be swum.

Lifted High

Riparian

Left alone. Let the word itself slide along
a corridor of flood plain
                    —*riparian*—
by the channel to the stream. Interface.

A bobble-filtered bottle bobs along the surface
above overflow from sanitary and storm.

A word in the mouth sidles in wet rushes over
the tongue to burst upon banks of the Thames.

Woodcocks drum in May at Kilally Meadows as
mallard mothers introduce their pride to water.

Cattails sieve sediment in the marsh. Let alone.
Carrying on. There a dead ash stands undercut by
spring current sweeping without resistance among
dangled roots. On topmost branch, the local osprey,
intent upon a shoal of suckers suspended in shadow,

catches sunlight, breast gleaming, before plummeting
with curved claws to pluck family breakfast.

Let word of mouth ripple (water ways) and ripen
on groves of wild garlic, on sedge, while svelte bank
swallows dart and swoop, chittering to one another.

Without us, the river would repair (itself) in time.

The Way Down

So many ways of endangering
a species. This one by
innovation, free enterprise
though evolution may flatline.

A Canada goose couple command
an old osprey nest atop the baseball
stand at Kilally. Vigilant of power as
in any new takeover

The male stands guard while mama goose
broods, proud of finding a ready-made
home, safe from prowlers. Location,
location, they honk.

Nearby a single osprey— perched on
another pole platform the city built to lure
osprey away from that baseball light—
makes a new nest with twigs.

My bet's on the goose to protect his home.
But what will happen to growing goslings
when they step out of the nest into sky? Nets, anyone?
Bird alert. Bird warning.

Not all innovations turn out well.
Small puffs of fluff will step into air from
their high perch as if
into water below.

But this blue will not hold. Wish such
fledglings were light as feathers
wafting on a slight breeze.

I fear
the plummet, the waiting maw of ground.

Ah, now I'm told
the chicks will simply flutter down and
as lightly land.

Tai Chi

The goose lately
is a little more
goose,

Prancing
aligned
to spring green,

Guarding
her first goslings.

At outer reach
wings fold,

glance through
our parallel
stretch.

Glimpses on the run. As in

a martial art
each move slips
by our shaping arms.

Alongside her alarm
we cluck her hiss away.

"Waving hands at clouds"

"Waving hands at clouds," I practise the wind-
mill move, tai chi, circulating ethereal currents

between my fingers as wave turns to cloud and
cloud to wave. The world turns, spinning a part

to despair and another on to be appreciated here.
Rolling the wheel, spinning the spoke of cycle.

Watching goldfinch alight, we witness spring
unfold. Green leaves creep from tips of redbuds

replacing magenta blossoms. Folding,
unfolding.

Born Aloft

Believe...

In the space of a year, Ula has learned to sit,
to stand, to walk, to totter forward in a run.

She has seen one full round of the seasons.
She wraps her family round her little finger.

Now just before dusk we stroll hand in hand
to witness the evening ritual of geese return.

Gliding along the Thames in formation, they
skim overhead, flapping slow time in synch.

She studies their procedure, dropping my hand
to edge forward, neck outstretched, arms aero-

dynamically angled. She flaps and flaps along
the bank, following their flight, ready for that

sudden lift. Again, again, till the last goose has
flown. Dragging her heels home, disconcerted,

she braces her body against the rising breeze,
bewildered that she too can't take off to sky

but game to try again tomorrow, convinced
the birds' secret will soon belong to her.

Bird Talk

Kai sprawls at eye level with a murder of crows
pecking at the ground for corn kernels. He
squints an eye and squawks as if conversing.

A crow he connects with cocks its head. Glad
to be understood, it caws responding plaint.

I place the robin redbreast with an injured wing in
a dish with a lid so that the darkness reminding it
of night will settle it down. In the homey gloom
with paper provided, it might reconstruct the nest

that blew down from its tree. When Kai in protest
removes the lid, the bird, frantically flopping its wing,
hops out of the dish and into danger under a bureau
near where the cat prowls on seductively soft pads.

Fluttering between dark and light, the robin awakens
out of instinct into confused flurry of panic that only
draws the cat's attention to uncertain outcome.

Little

Warblers no larger than
leaves emit songs louder
than I can bellow—

yellow in green bush
flickering in May mist
spectral among primary
mysteries of spectrum—

a chlorophyll trance
induced by light seduction.
The tree enticing light,
the water entrancing light.

Light mirrored and then
refracted into river shadow
where carp or suckers flurry
under bent-over willow.

Green smugly shines forth
having eaten pure light, its
rare performance renewed
when spring alights again.

Arrival

Goldfinch float above golden daffodils,
hang upside down on the stalk of old sun-
flower to catch last fall's last black seed.

A blaze of cardinal lilts down to settle on
clouds of creeping charlie, gill-over-
the-ground, and sky-blue forget-me-not.

Wasps and bumblebees scheming for nectar
dip and swim through the haze, yellow and
black, carrying home their burden of pollen.

Coming into Day

Where I know myself to be most true is in
this garden, listening to what plants need.

The Carolina wren awakens in dark before
five, brash and bright as its racing stripe.

This American tourist, here to stay with
global warming, visits the shed for possible
nesting site, darts to exit fast at our approach.

Outside, she churns out a peal that carries
across the yard, so much more piercing
than you'd think that tiny, flitting body

would allow. Sound reverberates what
tongue cannot repeat. Why is there such
a gulf between ear and mouth? If only

ear could descend to hear the heart and
utter her plaints in trills. A tuning fork

resonating with dawn, even as I rise al-
most reluctantly and gather garden tools
to work the ground, to open the heart.

Colour Bar

Orioles everywhere this year—
bright gleams searing the sky
impeccably orange and black.

A red-winged blackbird creaks
like a clothesline in low gear.
The river it nests by murmurs

bubbles of possibility, ignoring
frothing eddies of sodden soap
for the fun of funnelling spray.

Spring's annual utopia of hope
collides with dystopian detritus,
shoreline picketed by plastic.

At the FIFA Bird Cup

An oriole alights right beside
the plaintively chirping rose-
breasted grosbeak perched
on the cottonwood bough.

The grosbeak darts across
to a willow, followed swiftly|
by oriole. Both males are
dive-bombed by a fast female.

Her blur of colour matches rose—
white, black, and orange melée.
Grosbeak's dun mate in a feud
defends their domain, her brood.

Here/There

Three mother letters—
Fire, River, Water.

I find you in speaking
tree, pond eye,
river ear—

meadow's hand,
loop of swallow,
stream of thought.

There you are—
Ula in the pool,
strands of hair floating
as if on the Thames—

submerged but for her
smiling face. Ahhhhhh,
she murmurs

The mud bank from
which snapper drops,
splash of circling carp.

Duck with her brood
aligned behind her,
careful setting out across

the wide water,
strutting down the street
to the creek.

Hummingbird fast
as the letter Shin
on fire, on red
cardinal flower.

There you are green
again after drab dearth,
long absence of light.

There you are in moments
between friends, among
many.

There you are in the mouth
of another, tenor's laugh,
an operatic trill.

There you are in the ear-
receiving wisdom, at last
ready to understand.

There you are in those eyes,
riverine, opening out, trans-
mitting from mirrored depth.

There you are in a rose,
first bloom or faded,
faintly scenting the air.

There you arise full-blown.

You are also inside, inner, with me.
Radiance seen, felt, and heard

A whiff of this, aroma of that,
taste on the honeyed tongue.

There you are in the cardinal
feeding his mate. Garlic scapes
spring arabesques in the air.

There you are in the sudden
confirmation of synchronicity
when the radio speaks the word

I am writing. Jack Spicer, move
over. And keep talking, please,
humming through medium cool.

The song responds, corresponds
to mood.

Contemplate the missing, lost,
forgotten, ignored, left out.

Enough now. Let it be
enough.

Wild Crafting

My daily bouquet of dandelion
satisfies the neighbours' need
for desert of green grass and mine
for wild.

The yellow vibrant heads last
just a day, and then plunge sodden
into compost, to rot and feed more

flowers, not to go to seed and
propagate as they are raised to do.

Daily, the flowers bloom closer
and closer to the ground, as if

to speed the cycle, to seed before
the lawn mower lops off their
vibrant unmistakeable heads.

In thwarting their will to reproduce,
I celebrate their evanescent charm
and serve their leaves for lunch.

Solution

We two skalds sit together side by
each, looking out over centuries.

We watch the stirred pot settle till
murky situations sweetly clarify of

their own accord, attuned to an old
rhythm whose resonance is our song.

We watch the seasons' rush, leaves
deciding on whether it's spring or

fall. The creek is slowly turning into
pond, so water plants blithely tell.

And the frogs declare they're home.
They're not going anywhere else

now that our water levels equal
spirit level. Toads will return in

time to lay a million unimpeded
eggs, a myriad tadpoles and more

toads a fingernail long to bide a
while as *lares* in their garden lair.

"Turtle, Turtles, All the Way Down"

We are waiting for turtle to arrive.
She is taking her own sweet time.

But her pace is steady, her approach
sure. The earth gives way under her

tread, each clawed foot lifting, firmly
set through the clinging chaos of mud.

We who are waiting trace both history
and future forks in her track. We spell

out the auguries to be revealed and
revered while our spearmint tea cools.

Along the shore, a spiny softshell clambers
onto the open neck of sand, vulnerable,

her long neck stretched as in human
labour, the effort bearing no

consequence she will ever know
or recognize. Legs splayed over

gravel, she strains. And her eggs
stream into their shallow stone nest,

haphazardly protected by a thin layer
of sand flung by her flat flippers.

Biological destiny complete, she ambles
into the bush, not looking back.

"The sandy areas spiny softshell turtles need to
lay their eggs often double as hotspots for developers"

A flapjack slides off its griddle beach,
leading with its snorkel-like snout,
slipping into river as into fire.

Its leathery carapace flexible
enough to float a moment sun-
struck, before sinking into its own
domain of mud and waterweed.

All too many ways of endangering
a species. Who would have known
that sand temperature determines

most turtles' gender? Lately, females
predominate, given global warming—

but this turtle's hatchlings are sexed
"independent of incubation temperature."

Though females take a decade to mature,
they can live half a century in the wild if
they survive the threats from dam floods.

Lately, six thousand babies incubated in labs
were freed in secret spots along the Thames
to protect them from poachers and predators.

"Without this breeding program this species
would be completely lost," remarks a species-
at-risk assistant with the Upper Thames River
Conservation Authority.

https://www.cbc.ca/news/canada/london/london-spiny-
soft-shell-turtle-thames-river-1.4259280

Resigned to Propagation

Here we are. Here I am, the toad
sings, swelling his throat. Over here.

Who's to tell him he is ugly, spotted,
mottled, mean?

Not the great female who allows
him to mount, to ride her for a
day or two and drop his milt as

she deposits a creamy strand of eggs
and new tadpoles soon squirm.

Open

The hesitant moment
when tadpole loses its tail and
translucent legs appear, all

four, poised to quiver between
water and air, almost
ready.

It knows how to swim,
to climb out of brackish
water, to hop underleaf.

No turning back now.
No past encounters.
No future whims.

The power is all thrum
in a moment of transition—

The tadpoles huddle together, piled like
indeterminate cells that form a jellyfish.
They quiver in-between water and air, testing
the surface, capillary action.

Fully-formed toadlets hop out, off solitary in
long grass till next year's mating trill urges them
home to the pond where they were once strewn
in long lines of egg, till they wriggled free.

Tinier than fingernails, they bound
their way under jungle fronds, safe.

The grackles that nightly come to drink
at water's edge pay tadpoles or toadlets
no mind. Even the visiting duck couple
do not gobble them up. They must taste like

toads would taste, warty— I don't want to
think of adjectives, nor feel simulacrum
of toad upon reluctant blistering tongue.

Suspended Animation

Lolling in the swimming pool
between gray bloated cricket and
the fond hope of toad, a tadpole

not surviving chlorine infusion—
unlike its brothers we transported
by the bucket down to the Thames.

I turn amphibian, double-lidded.
Content beyond time to suspend
judgement of this lighter body,

beholding ongoing beauty without
human interference. Fit to strike
sudden tongue at inadvertent prey.

Of two minds among the elements
ready now for the river. The kids
and I carry tadpoles down in buckets.

Apantomancy

Apantomancy, they call it, and this turtle

    chances upon us deliberately
    on the margin of marsh—
bubble clusters bead the surface
    he breaks for air—

    gold eye at swamp level
      reptile-lidded both ways,
      black pupil hollow
        to ancient telling—

"Turtle, do you know the way to The Forks?
    Comfort us, speak—"

      He says nothing
though his mouth cracks open like a smile
      to snap bugs flitting.

    Sun lights upon water
    reflect/ refract pattern.

He enters obliquely
    at angle of incidence
    his denser medium home—
flippers push through seaweed strands—

Turtles wear their home upon their back,
familiar with deep div(in)ing.

We follow slowly sluggish with change
to unclean green, brackish water
rolling off our great horn shells.

At first we thought how awkward
to manipulate that weight
but swimming of course we're light
amphibians
adapted to both.

Between sleep and waking
we surrender to the littoral
manifold
where elements collide.

bubble clusters bead the surface

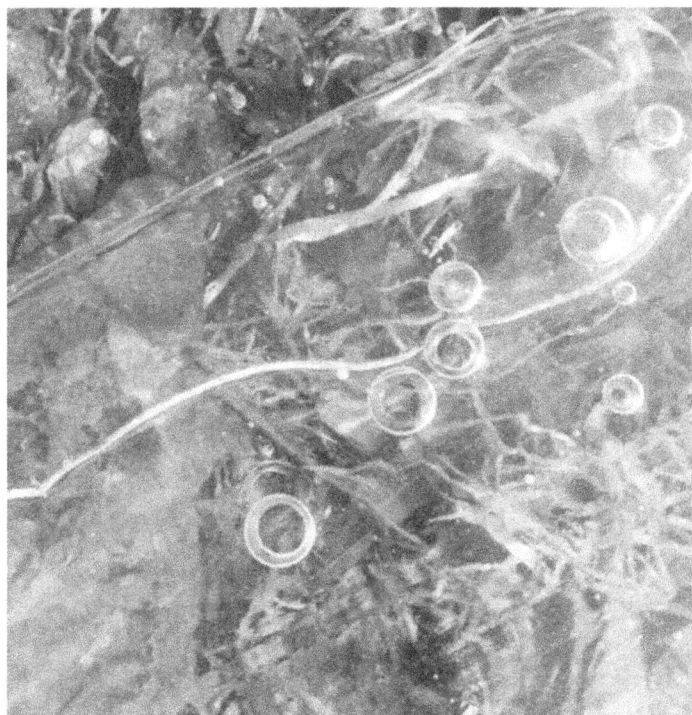

Evolution

Here's that water rat
left in a ditch where
it belongs. Bereft.

Not brought on board
our craft.
Leave it in the slough.

Slough it off like a worn
moth-nested coat.
Its small teeth are fierce.

Suspect its phosphorescent
reproachful eye, its cunning

squeal. Such bright cries
might conjure friends
of its own kind, who knows?

With time behind like wind
to cover surface lightly, it
might catch pace with our fast

sail someday, trailing litter
as wake. Why cling to stink
of fur when we could look

out to star, alert to start?

Pond Dynamics

Two toads are contesting territory with intermittent
trills. They have managed to scrabble atop a water
hyacinth or one of the planks set low on the surface.

There they squat, throats ballooning in male duel.
Whose pond is this anyway? There's room for both
but no. No room for more than one. That's the rule.

Listen up, children. The law's laid down.

Land Claims

Two male cardinals clash
more than colour against
our magenta redbud. Flick

of tail, darting branch to
branch. "I'm Alpha around

here. Get out!" I wonder if
they are brothers that forgot
last year's nest of fledglings.

Both claim their territory here.
Esau versus Jacob but no mess
of potage to swop. Swoop, flight—

they climb the ladder of sky till
one falls off, loops away to sulk,
hid in balsam fir till next round.

Grackle spies from birch bough.
A glimmer of speculation, what
can he gain from such commotion?

Catch and Release

Ula peers into the *Havahart* mousetrap where
a mouse hides under an enclosing steel flap.

We've caught the nighttime deer mouse in one trap
and a morning house mouse in another now. Ula is

fascinated by their difference in shape and behaviour—
feistily scratching against its bars or huddling shyly.

Before we release the mice into unsuspecting wilds,
Ula is drawing them. Off to let them go by the creek!

Pinned to our fridge door by magnet, by school pics,
her line sketch remains, reminder of living presence.

Rich as Stink

Elegantly understated
in Stella McCartney,

a skunk smooths her
delicate fashion under

the birdbath on a lawn
I'd thought was mine.

Let's share or rather return
property to its proper place.

The direct path empowered.

The must of her wake must
wake pheromones in her species.

Her presence so apparent, so
real a blessing as long as she

keeps that lovely fan
of swaying ostrich feather
down.

The Nature of Food

For weeks we fed five bereft baby skunks by Kilally,
a mixture of kibble soaked in mussel or tuna juice.

They hissed, tails up, but no spray, whew. No sign
of mother but the fading stench by the highway where
she must have been hit. No tomato juice for a while.

The babies were used to us, though I tried not to associate
myself with nourishment by leaving the tray unattended.

Let them learn to find their own grub. And at least one
did. Next season, a friend a mile off posted a photo of

a bold skunk in her yard by Stoney Creek. His V-shape
markings belonged to the alpha of the litter, the one who

was first to approach and snatch the children's offering
while his siblings hung back in their creche of river rock.

Among the Parasols

About us milkweed silk parachutes
dance. We catch the work, the word.

Light play patterns. How we toss to
and fro, expectant midway through

our lives. Almost mature, almost
coming into our own. Seed potency

bursting beyond hard casement,
through the boundary of design.

Surprised by Joy

Blessed be here. Blessed be clever cardinals
who vary their song into language only other
cardinals interpret. Blessed even be squirrels
who scold all intruders into submission.

Blessed be hostas and fern, mixing wild
with cultivated. Blessed be composted
soil that allows for splendid fluorescence.
Blessed be standing waves over the shoal.

Blessed be silent wing of crow and when it
lands on a spruce branch, that raucous caw.
Blessed be the interchange of story, space
to be alone together. Blessed be silence.

Blessed be the daily, the expanse of time.
Blessed be the dream. Blessed be night
that covers the shore in a moiré spread.

Blessed be the bare black cherry, dead
in winter's past blast but ready to turn
into fire's best wood, slow-burning,

Hot. Blessed be the fisher whose refrain
runs through a still too busy brain still
listening, listening to the river's flow.

Carp leap and fall, circling in stream.
Like calls to like through brightened air.

Winding, Unwinding

I spend hours every day bending the boughs
of honeysuckle, spirea, forsythia, and redbud,
weaving the limbs in and out around the fence
to simulate a clandestine walled garden of paradise.

Divining Ivy

As one friend calls to come collect
extra ivy for spring planting, I am
talking to the woman who introduced
us, talking of weaving, of braiding
collective communion of words with
such fine companions upcoming for
In Good Company, twin intertwining.

Winds Chime

Poets give voice to the voiceless,
the language we don't understand—

a breeze ripples throughout all
the aspen siblings down to roots
they share across a single source—

Sors, source, spring, sing sorcery.

A single tree may live a century in
clonal colonies while its system of
roots lasts millennia as the oldest

living organism. What would one
Trembling Giant whisper across
the river to its neighbouring clone?

"Hold on. Hold fast. Changing,
changing, elemental mingle," in slow,
shaky sibilants.

And silver leaves quake response.

Caving

Follow the cliff swallow
as she darts into her nest
down a round-ribbed hole
where her eggs wait for
that crack that opens new
dances, emerging possibility.

Look round when your eyes
make sense of the gloaming.
Satin pools glimmering
in reflected flashlight.
Silk spools unravel as you
travel down through story.

Spelunking is not a sport
to play without a rope to
pull you through. Cling to
Ariadne's thread— her clever
clues should see you out
the way we came but some-

how we know it won't be
easy. Night air removes colour
not with a swipe but gently. Light
withdraws, vanishes just as fireflies
start twinkling. Overhead, Venus
sinks toward the sun, each night closer.

The Birds that Flit at Break of Eve

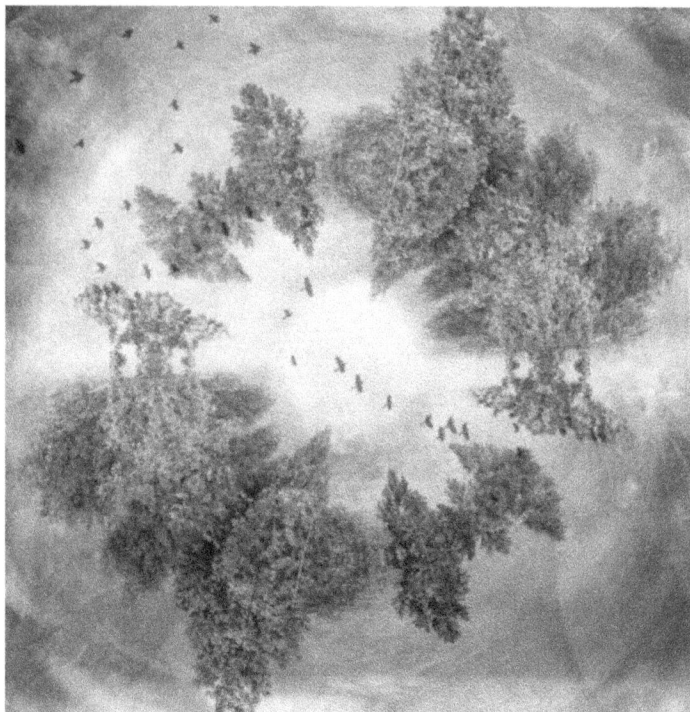

"It Dawns on Me"

The moment between
when artemisia silvers
from black to green,

slipping darkness off
for fresh daytime dress
as if as if green were its

constant, as if it did not
melt back at every close
into night.

Colour returns cautiously
as night noise disappears
and ghosts the dawn.

Hues arrive in morning dew.

Entrances

Cardinal is first to the feeder,
tssking his presence to remind
the morning glories it's their hour
to unfurl and blazon, announcing
London cardinal capital of Canada.

Entrances are everywhere, entrancing,
luring me to the ever realm of now
where somewhere I am always present,
waiting for my mind to remember and
sink down to ground, the simply true.

The past sways, shadowed by vague
remembrance, sways and looms in
the clearing by the creek. Looks to
the main chance to be heard again
right this time as rain left puddling.

There is more past than future for me.
But there's always time for beauty and
reflection, however muddy the water.
Though narcissus heads have nodded off,
the duty of such beauty is to bloom.

"Flowers Tell Their Own Time"

Mutative Metaphors

My lazy hammock dips and sways, paddled
with silver, dappled in sun yard, belying any
need for action beyond its own rhythm. I could
be brewing Earl Grey from bergamot leaf as
I drink lemon balm, peppermint, rosemary.

I could make tinctures to strengthen immunity out
of evening primrose and echinacea purpurea.
Or I could make Bach Flower Remedies from
impatience, chicory, clematis to ward off moods.

I could soak roses and heliotrope in oil for attar
or cream skin ointment from orange calendula.
I could stir-fry these glorious trumpet squash
flowers, stir starflowers of borage into salads.

But all that activity is for other years. Leave
valerian and foxglove growing unadulterated.
This garden I am lazily pleased to watch
parade its season and fall as though my gaze
were enough to bestow medicinal property

                    by osmosis, direct
through vision. Flowers tell their own time,
a continuous measure of light, soothing and
sequential. Before I lift a finger they are all
ready mulch. And next winter will have to rely
on my mind's eye for balm and taste's solace.

Names and memories on the tongue, exotic
dittany of Crete, Jacob's ladder, witch's vervain.
Instead for the garden and you, I offer only words
infused in a violet litany of properties. A river
of words on the Thames, floating downstream.

Bubbles arise when the hammock turns into
an old canoe, heavy-laden with drink and sun-
shade, heading around Big Bend, heading home.
jewelweed touch-me-not, rich globes of red
and gold catch and hold light along the bank.

Suddenly

Enter birdsong's particular tone or pitch,
an addition of whistle, glide, repeated chortle.
Enter wild-springing fern, growth of cedar.

Enter river's ongoing ripple breaking against
its bank. Enter sun, Midsummer Night's Eve.
Enter light, enter transmutation. Enter bud.

Enter purple garden of comfrey, iris, sage in
bloom. Enter rock, pitted limestone worn down
by water. Enter classic rock radio, workmen's

remarks. Enter heron and white-capped woman
stalking the marsh, her old black dog wagging
behind. Enter the bog, the margins of marsh.

Enter birchbark, paper pulled back by wind,
revealing sudden purity of inner white not
yet scarred by any brasher winter challenge.

Enter pine forest bath. Enter the squeal of
errant seagull, its patrol over shoals that last
year were islands, given higher water then.

Enter paradise enow, ongoing, unless we
chop down to make more mess, mcmansions
mushrooming. Enter hammock and sway.

Enter early summer and enter Experience
as Blake would have Thel do, and you.

Current

Flotillas of memory surface
floating, sinking again
through the seasons' current
currently.

Impressions painted later
on the fly, in the flow.

River runs. River falls.
River rapid. River torpid.

What the river carries
the river buries or casts
off shore. The littoral

remains, a line lasting
from season to season
of former beaches, long
lost. Like me. Like you.

Wishing Well

"I'm a river widened by misery, and the potency
of my language is more than human."
Terese Mailhot, *Heart Berries*

Something about truth, about
not needing belief or creed to
open up to all that is out there.

Blue sky is enough to take me,
or river. The thought so wide
it expands its own boundaries.

Beyond, beyond, so utterly be-
yond. Aspiration in action. To
become that whole, that full is

all I desire. A mon seul désir.

"The thing about women from the river is that our cur-
rents are endless.
We sometimes outrun ourselves." Terese Mailhot, *Heart
Berries*

Dependencies Depend on These

Negativity declined, I parse
a sparse part of light slid to
shadow all that last hour before

night gets hold of our bed and
shakes us down to sleep.

The far-off volcano spews and
we shiver in mid-August gloom.

No one can believe the rain
except the roses, bright glow of
abstraction while light lasts.

And I am still parsing, for that *ab-*
becomes *dis*, Dis of the underworld,
who appears in a field of hyacinth

for a distracted Persephone. Then
the night garden claims its colour
and all the blooms lie fallow. Only

sunflowers outlast obscurity, tow heads
still demanding a mother's attention
while the river rises, rises beside us.

From figure to ground to figuring out
the redolent darkness there's no mistaking
when even bright stalks fail, absent to sense.

The impassive eye receives, remembers.
We wonder what lone humans can change,
what dreams could spur us to act undistracted.

To Do No Harm

Slipping out of bed in early dream dawn, I wander down
to the river. There in shallows, something is slithering

between purple river weed fronds. An eel— a water snake?
They're not poisonous, are they? My own shadow cast on

the surface offers it cover enough to swim to shore. Waves
roll the snake into a weird kind of bird, ruffling the wet off.

A scrub brush serves as its back and tail feathers; its beak
a clothes peg. When I cluck, it nestles into a sand hollow,

unafraid. As I reach out to gather it up, it shifts shape into
an ordinary white hen with red wattles, escaped from pen

up the hill. A red rooster struts about us to protect the hen.
Though I fantasize Sunday roast, her throat is safe with me.

Silicon Valley
for Kai

Do you remember the days
when silicon was an element
central to sand, the sense of
grit between your toes by
the river just beyond the
reverberating slap of the old
screen against the door
jamb where wood never quite
met wood and was kept
together by hook in eye?

It was revolutionary then to
discover silicon also sprouted
in the segments of scrawny
horsetail that surrounded
the house as soon as sand
met any sort of soil. You'd
chew the stalk thoughtfully,
its brittle twist into saliva,
thinking dinosaur, this plant
alive at the same time and
huge the way the past is
thrown by a trick of light
projected onto shadow
out of all proportion.

Yourself the size of an ant
in a jungle of horsetail.

And then the thud of approaching
brontosaurus, its jaws dripping green

weeds the size of trees, its wet eye
unable to focus on anything
as small as you at eight.

What to Do When Bees are Few

To make a prairie it takes a clover and one bee,
One clover, and a bee. / And revery.
The revery alone will do, / If bees are few.

Bees are sadly far fewer now, dear Emily Dickinson, but
these days it will take more than revery to save our planet,
our province, our town. What is right action? What follows
hope? We write protest letters to ban Roundup. We march.

What to do when garden centres sell 'bee-friendly' plants
laced with hazardous insecticide levels? We search for a
neonicotinoid-free nursery offering pollinator-friendly
wildflowers, native old-fashioned flora—late blooming
asters, brown-eyed Susan, goldenrod, and wild bergamot.

We are entangled in the consequence of folly and greed.
Where do we take refuge? A walled garden, a river bank?
Where do we find ourselves, our freedom, in the ongoing
lurch between our own restoration and public offerings?

We bear witness but we cannot be excused until we change
the narrative, till we retrieve all the paradox of multiplicity.
We learn to live with the many complexities of community,
whether wild or sustained, whether municipal or country.

We learn respect. We learn to listen. We learn when to be still and when to move. Revery will no longer do but it's a start, the necessary pause before action we can trust— "Health Canada confirm plans to gradually phase out these pesticides"

Leaks

After daily thunderstorms overwhelm ancient sewers,
raw sewage pours through overflow pipe into rivers
and lakes, spewing "a toxic stew of used condoms,

plastic tampon applicators, and mounds of shredded
toilet paper along with a countless quantity of other,
unidentifiable solids" with no real-time monitor.

"Environment Canada does require municipal governments
to report annually how much untreated wastewater is spilled,
but settles for calculations that are based on computer models,
rather than specific data of actual events." Or reality checks.

I'd rather write paeans extolling the Thames' long vistas,
gently coursing along green pastures of boneset and yarrow,
wild garlic, Joe-pye weed. And the elegant curve of bridge,
expansive Gibbons Park draped by weeping willow elders.

Would you not rather celebrate the return of beaver and otter?
But we can no longer ignore the impact of slack urban plans.
Ecco-poetry is practical— may it incite us to bear witness.

https://london.ctvnews.ca/one-trillion-litres-of-sewage-
leaked-into-lakes-and-rivers-over-last-five-years-
1.4050309

Studies in Extreme

A summer of fire versus water,
trees and seas crying aloud and
orca mother drops her dead calf.

Attribution Science lets us know
that improbable events are twice
as likely, given human influence.

The signal of human intervention
exacerbated by rising temperature.
Risks are up even at local levels.

While Souwesto is inundated in
thunderstorms and rivers are high,
forests are flaming north and west.

People may be burnt out because
the future feels distant, but we are
already affected. This exceptional

hot summer will become the norm
unless we act on working solutions
now. Climate change is changing us.

Quirks & Quarks, August 11, 2018

The Reverie of Poor Susan

A nostalgic note in the city reminds Wordsworth's
woman of her former country life. Now we read in
the light of what we too have lost, as London eats
cornfields. Creeks are channelled into concrete
catchment basins, surrogate proxies for suburbia.

Once gone, who can recall the grove of mixed woods
or hills now bulldozed flat, the marshes sucked dry?
The land does not hold palimpsest of former glory but
memories float like fog above dun mushroom homes.

Poor Susan has passed by the spot, and has heard
In the silence of morning the song of the Bird.

'Tis a note of enchantment; what ails her? She sees
A mountain ascending, a vision of trees...
And a river flows on through the vale of Cheapside...

She looks, and her heart is in heaven: but they fade,
The mist and the river, the hill and the shade:

The stream will not flow, and the hill will not rise,
And the colours have all passed away from her eyes!

https://www.poetryfoundation.org/poems/45546/the-
reverie-of-poor-susan

Once

So Far Sitting Pretty
                    September 11, 2017

While Hurricane Harvey harasses Houston—
while Earthquake 8.2 devastates Oaxaca—

while Irma's eye widens over Florida Keys
and Trump advises, "Just get out of its way"—

while wildfires torch pine forests whole and
crossing continental divide, evacuate towns—

while Trump's toddler tantrums go nuclear
to defy Kim Jong-un's asinine missile taunt—

while race hatred rages in white supremacists
and America turns her tough back on Dreamers—

while refugees capsize in unforgiving, fraught seas—
while Britain's Brexit divides ancient allegiances—

while Buddhists slaughter Muslims in Myanmar
and women are executed in dishonorable killings—

while nightmares confront war game apocalypse
and brinkmanship totters on the edge of Equinox...

Then tomatoes gleam scarlet in the green of harvest
and hummingbirds linger in sun before migrating.

Caterpillar chrysalis becomes bright new monarch,
folding and unfolding stiff wet wings for first flight

while September shadows our yard in semi-annual
balance between light and dark. What to maintain?

We have read about that perfect summer of 1914
before the dam burst in bloody floods of war.

An azure morning behind twin towers sears us,
scorching flame gleaming on pure vertical white.

We do not know recompense. We try on equanimity.
In a world out of control, we are not without hope.

In a calm arising before catastrophe, we sit and wait.
Hope is left for last after all evils flee Pandora's box.

Sitting ducks, perhaps, yet ducks with luck, imminent
ingenuity, feathers still unruffled by looming storm.

We have our ways, small though they be. To evade
racoon plunder, we harvest reddening tomatoes to ripen indoors.

Return to Sender

September 11 has come and almost gone
again without new attack. The names recited.

We're wired to news without noticing the new.

A momentary equilibrium held like breath
in the balance. A turning point we hold as we

careen toward winter, one more turning point to
recall when Trump and cohorts bluster on.

The radio calls for a humidex over forty.
Stillness does not last beyond a moment.

Days of Awe and Hurricane

The autumn equinox falls this year mid-
afternoon in golden light, light suspended

over the bowl of time, suspended as mind
opens to a possibility of expanse, of hope

thought stupid— hope beyond thought, held
in the frame of wider events set spinning.

Our family of goldfinch flock to goldenrod,
twittering, tweeting, chittering at their feast.

Prince Harry breezes through Toronto traffic,
to celebrate Invictus, winners out of hiding.

Canada's "a work in progress," claims the PM.
Words do not replace realities. Mind the gap.

Mistaken identity and charges dropped but now
a bewildered refugee requires protective custody.

What we know we cannot say. What we don't
know fills the airwaves, as news ongoing, old.

Doctrine of Signatures

Seasons have their hues— ours is sun-steeped
translucence lit from within till it brims over.
Interjections interrupt a trail we conceive as real—

the present as gift, as presence, the only possible
way through, way in. Memories weigh in wedged
as if they were real. Futures impinge as if secure.

Females dun beside their bolder mates, gold-
finch cross the sky in graceful loops of liquid
flight and song, sway on green fronds that bow

under light weight to the doctrine of signatures.
Cedar or Bohemian waxwings twitter among
bare boughs on their way warmward.

Goldfinch, cardinal, dragonfly, all hightail it
on the updraft, waiting for wind to shift at the red
round of setting sun.

The flock alight and lift on a single breath. South,
south. Sweet wind, carry them safe in light flight.

Goldenrod scimitars flash solid arabesques of late
summer, late afternoon, late in our lives for such
luminous entrance.

Preparation of Monarchs for Migration

Big Bend, with no buteos in sight
but butterflies flitting off goldenrod
to overnight on butternut leaves.

A newcomer and the bunch flares
like red candles in the setting sun,
opening the veined leaves their wings.

A slice into ripe watermelon, sudden
crimson. Rise and settle, restless
before the long improbable trek

to Mexico, waiting for winds to shift,
hightailing South on the updraft.

All Hallows' in Tatters

Monarchs depart bedraggled
orange and black just in time
for the Day
of the Dead.

Who knows what
will make it?

All Souls collect these
frayed flight-weary
spirits to be
warmly
welcomed
home.

All Hallows' E'en
for Ian

While you were still embattled,
I dreamed you were wandering
in pyjamas out back, looking for
a way through, the way on or out.

Your sister tells me your intention
was to walk toward the mountains
as many are doing these days, for
your cancer is a journey, not a war.

Now you breathe ever more slowly.
You take a breath in and then, your
sister says, you don't breathe out.

The sky widens to receive you.
Stars embrace your ascent on
Samhain, fire festival. A wheel
of planets sings you free.

Your timing is impeccable but then
you always were on time. Now
you slip away a little after mid-
night on All Hallows' Eve

when the veil between realms
parts slightly to reveal more
dimensions than we guessed,
making it easy for you to return
when you wish, when we attend.

All day I have made ready
celebrating the fall
of leaves, celebrating sky,
blue against orange maples.

Not knowing it was your time
but feeling transition, a final
transformation, Ian, this E'en.

This evening I stroll by the water
through woods ghost-lit by light pollution
spread like fog. I meditate on limestone
blocks left by a bobcat's improvement.

Medway Creek ripples by, reflecting light.
Behind me, a tree shakes. A form emerges
out of stillness, solidifies into a familiar
presence, strong and still. You are here.

A buck rubs his antlers against the maple,
shearing his velvet, a rack of three tines.

He freezes as I turn round and stands,
a statue, while we regard one another.

When at last I rise, his silhouette
dissolves with the white flag of his tail.

His musk fills the glen. His absence lingers.
We've never seen a buck around here.

What has called you back after cancer
ate you down past bone? You belong here

once a year, rubbing against rough bark
sloughing the sore velvet of old skin.

These woods are your domain, not dark nor
deep. They're a fringe of flood plain by the creek.

You have no more miles before you sleep
past time.

Poem for an Elder, Turning, Returning

As she flows in and out, we wait.
Attending. Attentive. A tension.
What is to be paid? What owed?

The river is shallow for
November but its current
runs deep. Consciousness
flickers, will-o'-the-wisp only
altered by constant choice.

Sharp shards hold us close to
home since she is ninety-five
and almost ready to return.

Rain streaks our windowpane.
Valiant snapdragons reach for
the light we all must tend to,
tend toward. Rain condenses
just when thought dissipates.

The flurry of warblers has departed down
river, leaving bare limbs of poplar to winter
birds, bright streaks of blue jay and cardinal.
The osprey, too, have left with their fledglings.

We gather the last bouquet of snapdragons
for an indoor vase, attending the final phase.
For we can take nothing personal as we go.
She leaves with the wind. And we of necessity
let her go.

When Trees Speak

Fall Back

The season is changing. Water freezes
on the vine, drop by drop. November
drizzles. November sucks, remember?

Remember. The month to endure,
the one that gets away with if not
murder than mayhem more than May

ever would. Or wood not, now the trees
are dormant, not silent but not speaking.

Leaves hang bewildered still green on
branches, in-between states of rage or
age, unbecoming the real. Greys

thicken into cloud cover, condense to
snow first. Falling leaf in lonely dance
settles among peers upon the ground.

The sky is lowering, lowing like cattle
huddled in the grey corner of the field.

Life inside is bright, fluorescently bald
with our indignant enclosure, trapped
before winter glows sparkle and miracle.

"I am at a crossroads," you say. But will
not say any of the directions you might
head to. Headstrong. On a cross-quarter

night, darkness falls too early for all we
want to do outdoors so we turn on artificial
light in gratitude. Let the little shine long.

Convergence

Walking alone the river to slow my brain, I
watch a kingfisher loop over the ice, a silent
cerulean swoop. A bird of Venus, conjuring
august presence, descending on our river.

Last night I dreamed of kingfisher, perched on bare
branch of tree, regarding me, silent. Recalled Olson's
"Kingfishers": What does not change/is the will to change
He woke, fully clothed, in his bed." I got up, opened
Lyall Watson's *Gifts of Unknown Things* to a page

where the writer has just sighted a kingfisher and talks
of the Asian ability to hold intervals silent in
the space between sounds. Aha. So I don't need to ask
kingfisher to speak as would be my wont. Let Love
let go. Let Love make room for more in the open sky.

Candled

Snowdrops, Snow Dropping

Pale moon over fields and woods
shines on the Thames' murky waters

(from *Tamesis* or "the dark one",
an original Celtic or pre-Celtic word.)

A huge ring of cirrus cloud surrounds
this moon's sparkling round clarity.

Full blue and blood Moon in Leo
opposite the Sun in fixed Aquarius.

A lunar rainbow refracted off water,
droplets in the atmosphere, portending,

I fear, storms. Shivers down the spine.
This Tamesis wears a deep green cloak.

Snow, Snow

Under an ice-lace fringe
the dark river rushes clan-

destine nocturnal moves
beneath the silver moon.

I am wearing amber beads
and glimpsing their secret—

what is encapsulated, what
frozen within, evasive, elusive,

held still and taut,
taunting. A taste of melt on

the tongue, teasing, tantalizing—
who knows the depth of deception?

Today snow sat up and shook its feathers—
three geese at Arva Mills set on sunning.

Tundra swans have been spotted, thousands
to alight on snow melt by the marsh. Soon,
surely. Spring. Again.

Acknowledgements

I was first inspired to write about the Thames when taking part in the Kuhlehorn project in 2008. A group of local artists and environmentalists recreated painter Paul Peel's journey down the Thames in1877, with his mentor, William Lees Judson. Present day canoeists paddled from London's pumphouse to the mouth of the Thames. Our art show, "The Thames Revisited," was exhibited at 1st Hussars Museum in London. My own piece, "Apantomancy," is included here.

River Revery is part of a multimedia collaboration with Mary McDonald— commingling my environmental poetry on the Thames River, with Mary's photo art, music, multimedia animation, transmedia storytelling, and website, RiverRevery.ca. The project reflects our ongoing concerns as artists deeply involved with our particular place and cultural community by expanding print publication in employing innovative platforms. "Believe," by Mary McDonald, is one of the poetry films that comprise *River Revery*:
https://www.youtube.com/watch?v=FENBcHzcPUA&feature=share.

Mary McDonald and I gratefully acknowledge the support of the London Arts Council through the City of London Community Arts Investment Program (CAIP, 2018) for our project exploring the Thames. It's been a joy to work with Mary, whose imagination and skill are unbounded. QR codes in *River Revery* link to multimedia work, thus expanding the experience of poetry in exciting ways. Mary presented poetry films from *River Revery* in 2019 at Open Educational Resources Conference (Galway, Ireland); and Reel Poetry Festival (Houston, Texas). *River Revery* was introduced as a model for engagement, exploring the impact and potential of community participation in arts collaboration. *River Revery* was also shown at Newlyn Film Festival (Penzance, UK); London Central Library for Gathering Voices in National Poetry Month 2019; and Museum London during Wordsfest 2018.

Dennis Siren, a brilliant videographer at Saby Siren Productions, created the QR code for the opening poem, *River Revery*, filmed at London's St. Paul's Cathedral for Nuit Blanche. *River Revery* also opens my Sound Opera, *Re-Visions: a seasonal cycle of ecco-poetry*: www.youtube.com/watch?time_continue=20&v=jhQ7En IYa3M. This performance was presented at Aeolian Hall, London in 2009, with Anne Anglin, Ruth Douthright, John Magyar, Chris Meloche, Rob Menegoni, Brenda McMorrow, and myself. Many of these poems were first presented then. As Canada Council Writer-in-Residence for Western University, my project was the DVD, *Luminous Entrance: a Sound Opera for Climate Change Action*. The performance was recorded live, edited and designed by Dennis Siren, and published by Pendas Productions in 2011. Dennis's videopoem, "Among the Parasols," has been entered in several poetry film festivals. His new video will be included in Penn's forthcoming book of poetry, *Souwesto*, thanks to the 2019 Community Arts Investment Program (CAIP) from London Arts Council.

Harold Rhenisch has explored text from *River Revery* in intricate detail on several of his blogs: https://okanaganokanogan.com/2018/12/03/reading-penn-kemp-and-the-world-the-role-of-poetry-in-civic-planning/ and https://okanaganokanogan.com/2019/02/13/repaired-post-towards-a-new-cartography-part-3-the-strength-of-oral-story-telling/. They are extraordinary readings.

Several poems have been published in the little magazines that poets owe so much. "Wind Chines" is up on www.sageing.ca/sageing29.html. "The Colour Bar" is featured in *Lackadaisy*, Summer 2019, online http://www.lackadaisylitmag.com. "Land Claims," "Cured," and "Surprised by Joy" appeared in London's *Synaeresis* #4, October, 2018; "Waving Hands at Clouds," *Synaeresis* #7. Early versions of a couple of poems were published in *Dinosaur Porn* and *Goddess Pages*. Occasional lines have been excerpted from my books, *Barbaric Cultural Practice*, *Travelling Light*, and *Trance Form*.

Thanks so much to endorsers Diana Beresford-Kroeger, Nina Desjardins, Ann Kerr-Linden, Irene Mathyssen, Margo Ritchie, and Catherine Ross, as well as to kind readers Anne Anglin, Madeline Lennon, Harold Rhenisch, and Aliyana Ruekberg. As always, to my dear Gavin Stairs, who keeps the home fires glowing, and to my family, especially beloved grandchildren Ula and Kai.

Photo: Mary McDonald

About Penn Kemp

Poet, performer, and playwright Penn Kemp has been celebrated as a trailblazer since her first publication of poetry by Coach House (1972), a "poetic El Niño," and a "one-woman literary industry." She was London's inaugural Poet Laureate (2010-13) and has been granted numerous municipal, provincial, and national awards. Chosen as the League of Canadian Poets' Spoken Word Artist (2015), Kemp has long been a keen participant/activist in Canada's cultural life, with thirty books of poetry, prose, and drama; seven plays and ten CDs produced.

New poetry books in 2018 were *Local Heroes* (Insomniac Press) and *Fox Haunts* (Aeolus House). Forthcoming in 2020 is *P.S.*, a collaboration of poems with Sharon Thesen (Kalamalka Press). Recent plays have been performed and published celebrating London local hero, Teresa Harris: https://teresaharrisdreamlife.wordpress.com/. Quattro Books has published her poetry, *Barbaric Cultural Practice*, and an anthology, *Jack Layton: Art in Action*. pennkemp.wordpress.com, pennkemp.weebly.com, www.canpoetry.library.utoronto.ca/kemp and https://soundcloud.com/penn-kemp. Updates are on http://facebook.com.pennkemp.poet. Follow her on Twitter, Instagram (pennkemp) or https://www.facebook.com/pages/Penn-Kemp.

Photo: Kate McDonald

About Mary McDonald

Mary McDonald is a writer and multimedia artist living and working in London. Mary is committed to telling stories in ways that mix the arts: see marymcdonald.ca. In 2018, Mary launched an Augmented Reality art and multimedia animation exhibit, *The Dream Life of Teresa Harris,* in collaboration with Penn Kemp. This was for the launch of Penn's *Local Heroes* (Insomniac Press) at Museum London and in July at Eldon House Heritage Site. Mary is currently pursuing her Master's of Educational Technology through UBC. Follow her at marymcdonaldmixingthearts.

About Dennis Siren

Saby Siren Productions was founded in the year 2000. Our mandate is to document the 'Art Scene' in London, Ontario. We have produced extensive documentation of local artists, musicians, and poets. For the last decade, Saby Siren Productions has created videos for Penn Kemp's poetry as well as documentation of numerous live performances of her larger works.

Endorsements

"In *River Revery*, Penn Kemp pulls us into the natural yet mysterious realm of the water from which we came. Penn reminds us that the Thames River is integral to what has shaped our regional identity: Indigenous peoples gathered as community at the Forks of the Antler River, renamed the Thames by British explorers. A garrison was established at the Forks to secure the territory for settlement, and the City of London grew around the Thames' muddy, fertile banks. Penn writes that the river stretches back beyond memory and forward into the future. It is a world that has sometimes been forgotten, sometimes despoiled, but must be ever present in our consciousness as we reach to understand who we are and what we can become. I so enjoy the loving way Penn brings to life the life-giving nature of London's Thames in *River Revery*. The pictures are breathtaking. I am so grateful Penn and Mary love our river so much."
— Irene Mathyssen, NDP Member of Parliament for London-Fanshawe

"Penn Kemp announces that poetry is her defense against intrusive forces, where political exigencies collide with the environment. Poetry is her territory of hope. In this volume of poetry, Penn is not only the keen observer of life in the river and around the river. She is that for sure. More significantly, she is the enchanted interspecies participant and the lamenting witness of all that might be lost. The poems invite us into the ever-present realm of now, and the river as central motif holds both the

reassurance of ancient and slow movement as well as the results of the consequence of human folly and greed. The book itself is beautiful. The river and the poet remind us that there is always time for beauty and reflection however muddy the waters. *Riverrevery.ca* is a beautiful rendition: the artistry of it fits the artistry of the poem."
— Margo Ritchie, Congregational Leader, Sisters of St. Joseph, and lover of poetry

"Penn has a gift for the poetics of the personal and the archetypal as well as Ecopoetics. In this sorely needed book, she explores the River Thames with her grandchildren. She expresses her sharply indignant voice as an activist inspiring us to positive action in the environmental challenges and catastrophes we all face."
— Ann Kerr-Linden, host of Story Room Toronto

"The work as a whole has an insistence and urgency in the rhythm of its poems, very necessary now. *River Revery* feels like a meandering river with a stream-of-consciousness as if the reader is in the flow of a daydream or watching a movie from long ago."
— Nina Desjardins, rogue psychiatrist

"Beautiful! A lovely collaboration of text, images, and voice—and of course the River."
— Catherine Ross, Professor Emerita, Western University